The Best (& Worst) Jobs in
ANGLO-SAXON
& VIKING TIMES

Clive Gifford

WAYLAND

First published in Great Britain in 2015 by Wayland

Editor: Nicola Edwards

Designer: Rocket Design (East Anglia) Ltd

Illustrations by Alex Paterson

Dewey number: 331.7'009021–dc23

ISBN: 978 0 7502 8740 1

Library eBook ISBN: 978 0 7502 8741 8

10 9 8 7 6 5 4 3 2 1

Wayland, an imprint of

Hachette Children's Group

Part of Hodder and Stoughton

Carmelite House

50 Victoria Embankment

London EC4Y 0DZ

An Hachette UK Company

www.hachette.co.uk

www.hachettechildrens.co.uk

Printed and bound in China

All photographs supplied by
The Art Archive (www.art-archive.com)
except for p6 (t) iStock; p7, p15 (t)
Wikimedia Commons; p11, p12 (l), p14,
p16 (t), p18, p29 Shutterstock.com

CONTENTS

THE JOB MARKET
IN ANGLO-SAXON AND VIKING TIMES

So you're looking for a job in the times of the Anglo-Saxons or the Vikings? Good luck!

You are entering the era after the ancient Romans had left

Britain (in the fifth century CE). With the Romans out of the way, waves of different invaders and settlers came to Britain from northern Europe. These included Angles, Jutes, Saxons, Franks and Frisians who all arrived between 450 and 600 CE, mixed with local Britons and became part of what historians call the Anglo-Saxon period.

A small fleet of Viking longships sails towards England. During the first major Viking raid in 793 CE, Norwegian Vikings attacked and ransacked a monastery in Lindesfarne, Northumbria.

The Vikings were excellent craftsmen and wood carvers as this beautiful maple wood post carved into the head of a dragon shows.

From around 800 CE onwards, new waves of invaders from Denmark, Norway and Sweden, known as the Vikings, crossed the North Sea to reach Britain. These bloodthirsty newcomers first plundered places along the coast but later travelled inland and also began to settle in parts of Britain.

Both the Vikings and Anglo-Saxons were skilled and resourceful at using the natural world around them to survive, which led to some strange types of employment. Imagine spending all day heating wood in small pits to create charcoal in the hope of selling it to a blacksmith. To learn what other jobs you might find in these times, and which were the best and the worst, read on…

This Anglo-Saxon helmet was found buried in a giant grave at Sutton Hoo (about 15 km east of Ipswich) containing weapons and a 27-m-long wooden ship! The helmet was made of iron covered in copper alloy panels in the early seventh century.

ODD JOB

ANY OLD IRON

Some people eked out a basic living scavenging for bog iron — a type of impure iron found in muddy swamps and bogs. Bog iron hunters would have to wade through marshy ground, gather the foul-smelling lumps and then try to sell them to the local smith (blacksmith).

FARMER

- ARE YOU FIT, STRONG AND ABLE TO WORK ON YOUR FEET ALL DAY LONG?
- DO YOU HAVE PLENTY OF CHILDREN TO LEND A HAND?

Vegging out

Most Saxons and Vikings weren't bloodthirsty battlers. The majority were farmers who cultivated crops and looked after small numbers of livestock to provide food for themselves and their families. Many Saxon farms were open fields, split up into long narrow strips. Farmers grew crops including peas, beans, turnips and leeks as well as oats, barley and einkorn (a type of wheat), which they harvested using a curved metal blade called a sickle to cut the stalks.

Can't wait until school's invented.

Many Saxon farmers ploughed their field using a simple wooden plough which dug a furrow in the soil. It was often tough, backbreaking work.

Children didn't go to school but they were expected to work their family's land.

Meaty matters

If you were lucky, you might own some ducks or chickens or a handful of cows, sheep or pigs. It wasn't wise to get too attached to them or treat them as pets as they would get the chop when meat was needed.

The Anglo-Saxons might supplement the limited meat in their diet by hunting wild birds, hares and deer, but also slaughtered their own farm animals. Almost every part of the animal was used in some way with bone and horn turned into pins, needles and small tools whilst fats were used to make tallow for candles and lamps. The hollow bones of some birds were even used to make pipes.

A Saxon farmer's home was often small, simple, cramped and usually shared with a family's most prized farm animals. It was made of wood with a roof of thatched straw.

WORK MATES

DYING OF HUNGER: According to the writings of the Anglo-Saxon monk, Bede, some famine-stricken Anglo-Saxons in seventh-century Sussex made a suicide pact, all holding hands as they jumped off cliffs into the sea.

JOB VERDICT

A job for those with little ambition as there was no chance of becoming rich and every chance of becoming poorer and hungry if you suffered a bad harvest.

MONK

Life in the monastery

Early Saxon arrivals to Britain weren't Christians, but some later converted. Monks were Christians who devoted their lives to their religion, living away from the outside world in a monastery (see page 9). There, they each had their own room, albeit a tiny and bare one with few pieces of furniture or possessions. They were given free food as well as a free haircut, during which the top of their heads were shaved. The clothes they wore were usually undyed, plain tunics made of wool with a hood called a cowl.

(see page 9)

JOB VACANCY
Start date: 800 CE

- ARE YOU MALE AND A DEVOUT CHRISTIAN?
- DO YOU LIKE A BIT OF PEACE AND QUIET, AWAY FROM IT ALL?
- COULD YOU FOLLOW A STRICT ROUTINE DAY-IN, DAY-OUT?

ODD JOB

ON THE LOSING SIDE

Occasionally, monks fell foul of a savage king or nobleman. In 616, shortly before the Battle of Chester, Saxon king, Æthelfrith, had some 1,200 monks at the Bangor-Is-Coed monastery put to death because he believed they were praying for the enemy!

The monk Augustine preaches to Saxon king Æthelberht shortly after he arrived in Britain in 597 CE. The king converted to Christianity as did a number of Anglo-Saxons in his kingdom of Kent.

Prayers, punishment and plunderers

Monks were rarely idle. They were put to work looking after the monastery, working long hours in its gardens and lands, growing food, tending animals and chopping wood for fires, with frequent prayer breaks. Much-needed sleep at night was interrupted at 2 a.m. and again at dawn, for two more sets of prayers and woe betide any monk who slept in. Punishments varied from a severe beating to having to lie on the floor face-down for hours at a time. These punishments, though, could pale into comparison to the risks of an attack on the monastery by lawless bands or, in later times, by ferocious Viking raiders.

This painting depicts St Cuthbert, a seventh-century monk who is said to have chosen to cleanse himself by spending all night up to his neck in the freezing cold North Sea.

Shhhh, we're praying the Vikings don't attack!

JOB VERDICT

If peace and quiet and a rigid routine are for you, then life as a monk was good, providing you with food, shelter and work – just so long as a local king or raiders didn't attack your monastery.

9

SCRIBE

Copycats

Whilst some monks huffed and puffed performing all the hard physical labour, other monks helped build their monastery's library of books. There were no printing presses so the Bible, other religious texts and some works by ancient Greek and Roman authors were copied out slowly and painstakingly by hand. One book might take a scribe a year to reproduce and a single mistake would often mean that the page had to be started again. The work was carried out mostly in cold, poorly-lit huts and some scribes couldn't help jotting down their moans and whines, such as 'God. I am cold!' in their page margins.

A page from the *Anglo-Saxon Chronicle* produced by a scribe in around 891 CE. Scribes wrote on sheets of vellum made of calf's skin. Inks had to be home-made and used various recipes. Some mixed soot with the whites of eggs whilst others used rotting mushrooms, vinegar and even ground-up wasp eggs.

Most scribes copied others' works but one monk, Bede, became famous for writing his own, especially a five-book series about the history of England, completed in 731 CE.

NETTLE COLLECTOR

The sting's the thing

JOB VACANCY
Start date: 800 CE

- DO YOU LIKE THE GREAT OUTDOORS?
- ARE YOU GOOD WITH PAIN?

Stinging nettles were a commonly-used plant in the times of the Anglo-Saxons – and someone had to gather them. They didn't wear protective clothing to do this. They were more likely to rush right in to a thicket of nettles and grab as many as they could.

Getting stung was considered worth it, as the nettles were useful in a number of ways. The plant stems could be split and pounded to form a flax-like fibre which could be woven into cloth. The leaves were boiled in a pot or cauldron to remove the formic acid that was responsible for their painful sting.

Nettle tea was drunk by some Saxons and nettles were also used in medicine. An Anglo-Saxon medical text called *Bald's Leechbook* suggested using stinging nettles to treat muscular pain. Other remedies included using crushed nettles to treat constipation!

JOB VERDICT

A painful way to earn a living. Best avoided, especially without head-to-toe protection.

ANGLO-SAXON KING

In charge

Each group of Anglo-Saxon settlers had their own leader. A strong leader of a large group of Saxons might become known as 'cyning', meaning king. Each king in the early Anglo-Saxon era ruled over a small kingdom that was frequently battling its neighbours. The king was expected to lead from the front and impress with his warlike manner and skill in battle. As a result, job security wasn't great and many kings perished in conflicts.

Being a king in the later part of the Saxon era was a different experience. By 700 CE, many of the small kingdoms had been absorbed into a handful of larger kingdoms such as Wessex, Mercia and Northumbria. The ruler of these kingdoms wielded great power.

JOB VACANCY
Start date: 800 CE

* ARE YOU TOP DOG IN YOUR LOCAL COMMUNITY?

* CAN YOU LEAD YOUR FORCES INTO BATTLE SUCCESSFULLY?

* DO YOU LIKE BEING PRAISED AND FAWNED OVER BY OTHERS?

* ARE YOU SMART, CUNNING AND RUTHLESS ENOUGH TO STAY ON TOP?

King of Wessex from 871 to 899, Alfred the Great was a cunning military leader who fought the Vikings and later agreed peace treaties with them.

Law and disorder

A king in the later Anglo-Saxon era had a pretty good job. He commanded large lands and a powerful army. He could surround himself with hand-picked companions and bodyguards, all called thegns, and enjoy feasting and entertaining in one of a number of Great Halls he had built throughout his kingdom. But on other occasions, a king might have to be deadly serious and rule on Saxon laws. Some of these were extremely harsh; people as young as 12 could be sent to their death, while those who could not afford to pay a fine might be sold into slavery or have a part of their body cut off.

Some royal feasts were unruly affairs as the guests drank a large amount of beer and sometimes fought amongst themselves.

ODD JOB

WERGILD

In Anglo-Saxon law, wergild was a fine you paid for killing someone. Each type of person had a different price. In the Kingdom of Mercia, for example, killing a regular peasant or free man cost 200 shillings, a nobleman 1,500 shillings and the king, a whopping 30,000 shillings. If the person you killed was Welsh, then the wergild was only 80-110 shillings!

JOB VERDICT

The best job in Saxon times with lots of feasts and merriment – but watch out for rival kingdoms attacking your own.

EGG COLLECTOR

Eggs-tremely hard work

Spring could be a time of hunger and misery for **many Anglo-Saxons and Vikings.** They would have had to live off the food they had gathered and stored during the previous summer and autumn.

They would try to supplement these supplies by hunting, fishing or, for those who lived on some coastlines, stealing the large eggs of seabirds such as guillemots which nested on rocky ledges on cliff faces. Egg collectors would have to be brave, bold and athletic to climb down a cliff using a rope made of leather or seal skin armed with a leather bucket or woven basket to gather the eggs.

Attacks from outraged birds, razor-sharp rocks and the risk of falling to your death were all threats an egg collector had to deal with.

JOB VACANCY
Start date: 800 CE

- HAVE YOU GOT A HEAD FOR HEIGHTS?
- ARE YOU BRILLIANT AT SCALING TRICKY ROCKS AND CLIFF FACES?
- CAN YOU PUT UP WITH THE STENCH OF BIRD DROPPINGS?

JOB VERDICT

Only a suitable job for the gambler and adventurer, but if you were successful the eggs you collected would provide you and your family with much-needed protein.

GRAIN GRINDER

Daily bread

Bread was a staple part of the Anglo-Saxons' everyday diet but only in some larger settlements were there dedicated bakers. The women in most Anglo-Saxon families were expected to grind cereal grain to make flour every day or two. Grinding was backbreaking work using heavy flat stones called querns between which the grains were crushed. After several hours of grinding, the resulting flour was mixed with water, kneaded into a dough and baked in a fire pit or an earth oven to form a tough flat bread. Imagine doing that every single day!

JOB VACANCY
Start date: 800 CE

- ARE YOU A WOMAN?
- CAN YOU ENSURE BACKBREAKING WORK DAY AFTER DAY?

Grain was placed onto this large quern stone and then ground using another stone known as a handstone.

Most food in Anglo-Saxon times was cooked inside houses like these over an open fire. Bread was an exception as it was baked outside.

JOB VERDICT

Dull, repetitive work with low status, but the only way to make a family's daily supply of bread.

15

SMITH

Smiths in Anglo-Saxon times worked iron to make a wide range of useful things, from nails and knives to sickles for farming, axes for chopping and swords for fighting. The smith would work over a blazing hearth or furnace filled with a large fire. Into this he would force extra air using a pair of bellows to raise the temperature as high as 1,000°C. Iron heated to such temperatures stayed soft and malleable for several minutes, during which it could be hammered and shaped. An object had to be repeatedly heated and shaped before it was finished. Shaping included punching holes in the soft metal or hammering it to a fine edge for a blade.

JOB VACANCY
Start date: 800 CE

● ARE YOU STRONG, WITH ENOUGH STAMINA TO POUND HOT IRON ALL DAY LONG?
● DO YOU LIKE YOUR WORKPLACE TO BE SWELTERINGLY HOT?
● ARE YOU KNOWLEDGEABLE ABOUT IRON AND OTHER METALS AND HOW TO WORK THEM?

Anglo-Saxon smiths often made prayers or offerings to the god of smiths called Wolund or Wayland.

Many smiths were also skilled at working iron and bronze into highly-prized decorative items such as this goblet.

JOB VERDICT

As a smith, your local community needed you and you would have high status, especially if you produced excellent tools and sharp blades. You could expect burns and rough callouses on your hands from all your hard work though.

MINT WORKER

After the Romans left Britain, people mostly stopped using coins. Instead, they swapped or bartered their goods and services. The Anglo-Saxons reintroduced coins and these were made in metalworking centres called mints. Working conditions, like those for other metalworkers, could be hot, grimy and unpleasant. For many of the mint workers, who simply stamped an image on hot discs of metal (usually silver or silver mixed with a little copper) to make a coin, the work could also be deadly dull. Pay was often low or non-existent with the coin workers just receiving food and somewhere to live.

This hoard of gold coins known as thrymsas or scillingas (shillings) were made in the seventh century CE and re-discovered in Hampshire in 1828.

ODD JOB

BE WARNED

There were horrific punishments for those who gave in to the temptation to steal the finished coins or the silver used to make them. Some thieves had their hands chopped off which were then nailed to the door of the mint as a grim warning to others.

JOB VERDICT

A dull but not a bad job as Saxon jobs go for an honest worker – but those who couldn't resist stealing could expect a terrible punishment.

COOK

Butcher, baker and meal maker

Almost all cooking in Saxon and Viking times was performed by women at home. In many small homes, there were no windows, at most a simple opening in the roof acting as a chimney. This meant that the room would fill with smoke from the hearth in which blazed what Vikings called *máleldr* (meal fire). Above the fire was suspended a large cauldron made of iron or soapstone in which most meals were prepared.

You would need to be as much a butcher and baker as a cook to feed a Saxon or Viking family. Bread accompanied many meals and had to be baked regularly, while animals had to be skinned and meat prepared before cooking – not a job for the squeamish.

Small cauldrons hanging from metal tripods like these were often used by travelling Vikings looking to trade or invade.

[Master] Chefs need not apply

As the cook in a Saxon or Viking home, your head wouldn't be filled with dozens of fancy recipes. Meals were similar and based on what ingredients were available. Daytime meals, for example, might be a form of lumpy porridge made of cereal grains, sometimes with small amounts of meat and vegetables added. Dinner would be something similar, or a stew containing a mixture of meat and vegetables which was left bubbling for hours. Sometimes there were freshwater or sea fish to eat. These were either cooked in an iron pan or wrapped in leaves and baked in the ashes of the fire.

ODD JOB

FISH CRACKERS

For Vikings located further North, cod and other fish were sometimes dried so that they were rock hard and then eaten raw just like a cracker, even spread with butter or soft cheese!

Food was cooked in skillets like this one and usually served in wooden bowls to be eaten with a spoon, knife or with the fingers.

JOB VERDICT

A relentless and demanding job, especially if you were cooking for a large family, but with some (unpaid) satisfaction at making a meal well.

VIKING RAIDER

Fighting chance

As children, Viking boys often **learned the basics of wrestling and fighting using wooden weapons.** As adults, some Vikings made raids on lands throughout northern Europe, killing anyone in their path and stealing anything of value they came across.

WORK MATES

BERSERKERS: Some Viking raiders worked themselves up into such a mad fury before an attack, they were known as berserkers. These fearsome warriors believed they were invincible, often removed their armour and wore clothing made of bearskin as the bear was associated with the god of war and battle, Odin. To peaceful villagers under attack, they were terrifying.

Raiding parties were made up of a number of longships packed full of volunteers, mostly young men who didn't own land but who thirsted for adventure and a share of the spoils. Each raid was usually led by a chieftain or jarl (see pages 22-23) who was in charge of the treasure looted from a church, monastery, village or other settlement.

This ninth-century picture stone from Gotland in Sweden shows Viking warriors fighting and raiders in a longship.

Attack, attack, attack!

Viking raiders were often brutal, overpowering and very smelly as they carried no change of clothing for weeks or months at a time. Each raider might use a spear or battle axe (see below) in attack, and many wielded their most prized possession, a long iron sword.

One common tactic was for raiders to form a wedge-like shape with the best, most experienced warriors at the front. This was known as *svinfylking* or swine formation after the shape of a boar's head. Most raids were quick hit-and-run affairs, attacking, stealing and leaving before help or reinforcements could be summoned.

Many Viking raiders carried a wooden shield and wore a helmet without horns made of iron plates fitted together and often with a chain mail neck and throat guard. Some Vikings wore armour made of stiffened reindeer leather, but wealthier Vikings protected themselves with *byrnies* – tunics made of iron chain mail.

Many Viking longships were just 2-3 m wide and around 18 m long. They were powered by a square sail and sometimes rowed by the raiders using long wooden oars. They had a shallow hull which allowed them to get up close to shore.

JOB VERDICT

A high-risk occupation with the risk of shipwreck and death in battle, but with the chance to obtain great status and riches if your raids were successful.

JARL

Top class

Jarls were wealthy nobles who were the highest class of Viking society. Below them were artisans, traders and free men known as kralls or karls, while thralls – slaves mostly captured in battle – were forced to serve a master. A jarl might keep a number of slaves to tend the large hall made of timber where he and his family lived and feasted on rich dinners of many courses. Some jarls led Viking raids to foreign parts, but many stayed at home, surrounded by followers who acted as bodyguards and advisors and with workers to look after the land and crops.

A typical jarl's hall was longer and larger than an ordinary Viking's home. It was covered with a roof of thatch or turf.

WORK MATES

POETIC JUSTICE: Skalds were professional poets who would visit a jarl's hall and recite long poems from memory. Entertaining a jarl and his rowdy friends was no easy matter, so many skalds would make up a poem called a drapa full of praise for their host. If their work went down well, they could expect to receive a lavish gift from the jarl.

Some of the large collection of Viking coins and jewellery, made of silver and gold, found at the Viking settlement of Birka in Sweden and dated to 830-850 CE.

Many jarls hid their treasure in rocks or pits rather than display it in their home. Archaeologists today sometimes uncover one of these treasure hoards containing fine jewellery, swords and household items made of silver and gold.

Keeping everyone happy

As a jarl your main responsibility was to your followers. You had to help look after them, ruling over any disputes between families, and grant them treasure or land to keep them happy. Failure to do these things might lead to a group of followers trying to overthrow or even kill a jarl. A fine funeral was guaranteed for any jarl who could keep hold of his wealth and power until he died. The most powerful jarls were given a spectacular send-off. The body was placed in a burial ship which was set alight and launched onto the water to blaze away.

JOB VERDICT

Being a jarl was one of the very best jobs to have in the Viking era, especially for those who could keep their followers happy and stay safe.

VIKING TRADER

Ship to shore

Viking traders ranged far through Europe in their quest to buy and sell goods to make a profit. They sailed using *knarr* cargo ships, propelled by sails, most of which had a hole in the centre of the deck to provide more storage for cargo. Life onboard ship could prove harsh and cramped. There were no cabins and sleep had to be grabbed on deck. When a ship was following a coastline, it would moor at night so that the crew could sleep on land and gather any fresh food and water they could find. On the ship, food stores mostly consisted of dried fish and meats. Traders and their crew were understandably keen to get to their destination…and fast!

When traders were paid in local, foreign coins, they were interested less in the value of the coins than in how much silver they contained.

A *knarr* was broader and stouter than a Viking longship with a 5 m or so wide hull in which lots of goods or materials could be stored.

Profitable cargoes

Traders would buy a cargo such as fox, bear and otter furs, amber or whalebone and walrus ivory from Scandinavia and then sail to another part of Europe to sell their wares. Most prized were silver, spices from Africa and the Middle East and glassware from Italy and elsewhere. Traders also bought and sold foodstuffs such as wheat, wine or salt or materials such as wool, linen or tin. The aim was to make a large profit and avoid the attentions of pirates and swindlers in order to pay the crew and buy supplies and a new cargo for the next journey.

Greenland
Iceland
Norway
Sweden
Russia
Britain
Denmark
Germany
France
Newfoundland
Spain
Italy
AFRICA

The Vikings proved epic sailors and established trade routes all over Europe. They even sailed down rivers through Russia as well as reaching North Africa and Newfoundland in their ships.

Many smart traders took their own scales with them to weigh jewels and precious metals.

JOB VERDICT

Exciting and potentially profitable. There were plenty of threats to your success, but if you managed to repeatedly buy and sell well on your travels, you could become rich.

JEWELLERY MAKER

Budget and luxury

Men wore almost as much jewellery as women in Viking times, from shoulder brooches which fastened a cloak to elaborate belt buckles, arm rings and rings on their fingers. Most was fashioned from metal by jewellery makers, working in copper, iron and bronze for their cheaper products and silver and gold for their finest. Only jarls and other wealthy people could afford gold, although some traders bought gold jewellery so that they could carry all their wealth with them on trading trips.

JOB VACANCY
Start date: 800 CE

- DO YOU HAVE REALLY GOOD EYESIGHT (AS SPECTACLES HAVE NOT BEEN INVENTED YET)?
- CAN YOU STAY PATIENT AS YOU PERFORM THE SAME TASK FOR HOURS AT A TIME?
- ARE YOU BRILLIANT AT WORKING WITH SMALL, FIDDLY THINGS?

One of the most popular charms was the hammer wielded by the powerful Norse god, Thor. The hammer, known as Mjölnir, was believed to be able to level mountains.

This delicate gold brooch is made from gold wire shaped into patterns. Many brooches were also decorated with amber and garnets.

This charm is shaped to look like the Norse goddess of love and beauty, Freya.

Smoke and pig fat

Jewellery makers' fine pieces were produced in far from pleasant working conditions. Their huts would be swelteringly hot and filled with thick, choking smoke from heating and working metals. Their hands would be covered in burns, cuts from dealing with sharp metal, and pig fat. This was used to hold thin strands of wire in place as they were twisted to form complex designs. One slip up and a clumsy jeweller might have to start all over again!

This Viking jeweller's mould is made of clay. Hot, runny metal would be poured into the mould which set solid once cool to form these tiny charms.

JOB VERDICT

Mixed. On the one hand, you had the pleasure of creating artistic designs, albeit for other people to wear. On the other hand, you would have to work long hours in tough working conditions.

EXPLORER

Sail away

Many Viking traders sailed long distances, but some sailors went further. They pushed their sailing ships and crew into taking a leap into the unknown. The Vikings had no compasses or maps of the regions they were to explore, but were skilled sea navigators. They used the position of the sun and stars, the winds and flights of sea birds as guides. Ships would have been packed with provisions including wooden barrels packed with butter, cheese and dried meats. Some ships would have carried live goats and cows for milk and meat as well as chickens for eggs, all crammed on board.

JOB VACANCY
Start date: 800 CE

- CAN YOU SAIL A WOODEN SHIP AND NAVIGATE THE SEAS EXPERTLY?
- ARE YOU VERY COURAGEOUS AND SINGLE-MINDED?
- CAN YOU CONVINCE A CREW OF TOUGH VIKINGS TO FOLLOW YOU?

This gilded bronze weather vane was mounted on a Viking ship and indicated the direction in which the winds were blowing the vessel.

Finding new lands

In the ninth century, Viking explorers reached and settled Iceland in the North Atlantic. The following century, explorers such as Erik the Red reached Greenland. Some Vikings settled there, growing quick to mature crops such as barley and rearing hardy livestock. Although bitterly cold, the coastal areas of Greenland contained birch trees for firewood, while the waters were rich in fish, walruses and seals. Walrus ivory became an important trading product. In the late tenth century, Vikings voyaged even further west reaching Baffin Island and Newfoundland in Canada, 500 years before Christopher Columbus's famous trip across the Atlantic Ocean.

ODD JOB
FIERY FUNGUS

Ingenious Viking explorers carried fire with them in the form of the touchwood fungus. This fungus from tree bark was soaked in urine for days and then pounded into a felt-like material. When it was lit it would smoulder for weeks at a time, giving Viking travellers a portable source of fire.

This statue in Iceland depicts the son of Erik the Red, Leif Erikson. Historians think he sailed to North America from Greenland in the late tenth century.

JOB VERDICT

No one knows how many explorers perished trying to find new lands, and it was certainly a very high-risk business. Those who were successful were hailed as heroes.

LEIF ERIKSON
DISCOVERER OF AMERICA
1000 A.D.

QUIZ

Which job in Anglo-Saxon and Viking times would you be most suited to? Answer the questions below then turn the book upside down to read the verdict!

Questions

1 **Are you good at following strict orders and routines?**

a) Sometimes. I can follow instructions when necessary.

b) Yes, I much prefer to be told what to do and when. I like a routine.

c) No! I much prefer doing what I want and giving orders to other people.

2 **Do you like to travel a lot?**

a) No, travel doesn't interest me that much, apart from the odd trip to the market.

b) Definitely not. I do not much care for the outside world.

c) I like to travel but only if all my needs are looked after.

3 **Do you like physical activity and don't mind noise?**

a) Yes, I'm strong and can keep working hard for hours. Noise doesn't bother me.

b) No, I prefer peace and quiet, a little gardening and some reading.

c) I like some physical activity but prefer to tell people when I want quiet.

4 **Are you patient and good at working with your hands?**

a) Yes, I'm excellent at making things and using tools.

b) I am fairly patient and reasonably good with my hands.

c) No, not very. I prefer to get people to do things for me.

Answers

Mostly As
It might be that you are most cut out to be a Saxon smith or a Viking metalworker.

Mostly Bs
A life in the monastery might suit you best, either as a regular monk or a scribe, copying out written works.

Mostly Cs
Sounds like you're holding out hopes to be a Saxon king or Viking jarl. Good luck!

Glossary

bronze An alloy of the metals tin and copper, commonly used as a material in metalworking.

callouses Rough, hard skin often caused by frequent rough work.

cultivate To prepare land, sow crops and tend them as the plants grow.

impure A substance that isn't pure but instead, contains other substances mixed in with it.

invincible Too powerful to be defeated or overcome by others.

jarl A Viking noble or chieftain, usually wealthy and having power over a local area and group of people.

longship A type of ship built by the Vikings which was long and narrow to move quickly through the water.

monastery One or more buildings used to house a religious community of monks.

painstaking An action or task that needs careful and thorough work for it to be successful.

ransack To go through a place, searching for and stealing possessions as well as often causing damage.

supplement To add to and improve something, such as a person's diet.

volunteers People who freely choose to do something rather than being forced into it.

Further Information

Books

What They Don't Tell You About The Anglo-Saxons – Robert Fowke (Wayland, 2014)

Men, Women and Children In Anglo-Saxon Times – Jane Bingham (Wayland, 2011)

The History Detective Investigates: Anglo-Saxons – Neil Tonge (Wayland, 2014)

History Relived: The Anglo-Saxons and Vikings – Cath Senker (Wayland, 2013)

Viking Life: Invasion and Settlement – Nicola Barber (Wayland, 2013)

Websites

http://www.britishmuseum.org/explore/cultures/europe/anglo-saxon_england.aspx
Examine lots of different Anglo-Saxon artefacts at this British Museum website.

http://www.historic-uk.com/HistoryMagazine/DestinationsUK/AngloSaxonSite
Check out this interactive map of the most exciting locations in Britain or Anglo-Saxon life.

http://www.staffordshirehoard.org.u
Find out about the Staffordshire Hoard – the largest collection of Anglo-Saxon gold objects ever found.

http://www.bbc.co.uk/schools/primaryhistory/vikings
Learn more about who the Vikings were and their achievements at this BBC website.

http://www.hurstwic.org/history/text/history.htm
Find out about the Viking's weapons, trade routes and religious beliefs at this handy website.

INDEX